N. 8.

Concerto di...

Allegro aperto.

Del Sig.r Cav.e Amadeo Wolfg. Mozart
nel gennaro 1776 à Salisburgo

# LISTENING THROUGH

# LISTENING THROUGH

*Twenty-seven Concertos for Piano*

by Johannes
Chrysostomus
Wolfgangus
Theophilus
MOZART
*called Amadé*

## Robert Kelly

Contra Mundum Press    New York · London · Melbourne

*Listening Through*
© Robert Kelly

First Contra Mundum Press
Edition 2025.

All Rights Reserved
under International &
Pan-American Copyright
Conventions.

No part of this book may
be reproduced in any form
or by any electronic means,
including information
storage and retrieval systems,
without permission in
writing from the publisher,
except by a reviewer who
may quote brief passages
in a review.

Library of Congress
Cataloguing-in-Publication
Data

Kelly, Robert
Listening Through /
Robert Kelly

—1st Contra Mundum Press
Edition

148 pp., 6 × 9 in.

ISBN 9781940625799

  I. Kelly, Robert.
 II. Title.

    2025941325

# LISTENING THROUGH

*As composers set poems to music,
here I presume to set music to words.*

(LISTENING THROUGH)

Listening through, it's gazing into a diamond. It's staring into the fire. It's solitaire. It's staring with your ears, listening with an empty mind, being willing to be shaped or spoken by what one hears. It is irregular. It is illegitimate. It is, in my experience of it, breathlessly hurried, and like most urgent things, it seems dangerous, scary.

I'm trying to describe what I mean by 'listening through Mozart.' Or whoever it might be, the composer whose work I infest, or am infested by. I've listened through twenty-seven Mozart piano concertos — played by Murray Perahia, a set of CDs I happened to have. And I've listened through Shostakovich quartets, Biber sonatas, Bach partitas. Sometimes the music finds me a story that has to be told, sometimes it instructs me in verbal, grammatical operations that might (in some other world) be the equivalents of the musical gestures. Event for event.

My procedure is simple. Start & stop. I put on earphones to focus the sound source. I start a track on a CD or tape. I begin to write as soon as I begin to hear. I write whatever comes into my head, listening. So listening, like most beautiful things, is divided: I'm listening to the music and I'm listening to the words roused, rising, in my head. I'm listening through the music to the words in my head, listening through them to the music.

The two sounds mingle, interact, intercourse, get in each other's way, sing together, sleep together, sometimes resolve. How do I know what they're doing, I'm too busy writing it all down.

That's what I'm doing, I'm writing it all down. As long as the music keeps sounding, I keep writing. As soon as the music stops (the track ends — I move track by track here, accepting the mechanism that delivers the music to us in these days), as soon as the music stops, I stop.

That's it. There's not a hint of analysis, history, performance commentary, discussion, understanding. It's just standing under the music, listening to what it makes me think.

What it makes me think and what it makes me say. I don't know what I've heard, I scarcely know what it's made me say. I stop writing and look up into silence. Silence is usually in the shape of a window, with light in it, coming in. As it happens, I almost always face east, like a good Sufi.

It's staring into the fire till shapes appear, burning cities & black seas, faces, faces you think are in hell, but then they smile with a peace and clarity you've hardly ever known. It's staring into the keen blue blaze deep inside a hand-cut old diamond until that single point opens out as a road and you follow it.

Of course I write with immense gratitude to J.C.W.T. Mozart, H.I.F. von Biber, D.D. Shostakovich and the other geniuses I have allowed to puff along the

frail craft of my wit. They have said everything to
me, and I have perhaps said nothing at all to them,
or about them, or about their works that have been
so compendious with delight and instruction for
humankind.

No analysis here, not even any response to the specifics
of the piece. Just the raving gratitude of what I have
been all my life, a grateful but talkative listener. Don't
talk while you're listening! people used to tell me.
In vain.

*First listening: 10 December 2006 – 3 January 2007, Annandale.*

*Final version completed, 9 June 2007, Cuttyhunk Island.*

# 1. K.37

Scratches on ice
ice. History
is something to eat
with the fingers.

At least it clears the mind
but what mind?

every child
is a single question
it is the teacher's
business to ask

Three judges sit in a row
reading what they hear

pricking their papers with ballpoint pen.

Faster the wind
the examiners
hunt through the town for us
streets are for hiding in

lock the house of study
crows nearby
on the pear tree by the window

open summer prayer.

## II.

The eye goes out
from the sleepy wordiness of praying
to sit with the crow a while
caress the alert iridescent gloss
a commentary
of what your lips are saying.
Midrash.
Every word I ever wrote
is for you

and a man brings
so many and so many
to comment on

so sky and so wing and so word
a brick wall holds
suspended or enclosed

a house is always in a hurry
only the street
knows how to sleep

then the quiet comes,
the domes of ever.

You think because you wear blue socks
or scarlet underwear you
add a worthwhile footnote to
all the mischief going on

a tree with a headache
a bird with strange powers

with a little piece of wire bent.

## III.

But come now, o soft sweet then,

you wait for all my maybes

to tumble out of Moses's bed
and seek my Miriam

time waits for everybody
cruel illusion that it runs

nothing changes
it stands and we drown in it

stagnant time.

A swamp or standing pool
such as at life-end an oarsman
in his iffy gondola skims

so I have turned my back on time
and done when young what men do old

and let all of your hurry your hocks
kiss my whiskerlessly cunning lips

Attention never not pays.

## 2. K.39

One time I found the man asleep         *John Cage*
his mind studying the score or the screen
his sunburned neck
the tower beside the sea

Silence also is allowed.
Silence is a solemn ceremony

so there's room to dance around,
I hear my hand around her waist

I hear her to me,
it is the old fashioned thing the two
half afraid to smile the two
saying close things to each other
in Bickford's at dawn, New Bedford,

a cheek on someone's shoulder's
the eleventh commandment
and all the other ten dissolve in wine

he said, so what is two
it takes so many to say?

so many marks on paper
to say what you already know.

## II.

Maybe too many
mistakes the priests
are coming,

with all their frivolous
white dresses over fusty black
what do they want with
all of me?

They also peddle
a kind of beauty

though the will to rule
turns the sky to marble

our beautiful religion
all stone in the sky

but they rule like marble
in the sky's name

1. All Power to the People means All power to me.

2. Capital and labor both deride the mind

3. Money means to rescue you from what things really mean,

*tha-mal gyi shes-pa*, the ordinary mind,
the mind before you were you,
before you you thought you were there to think with it.

Mind always here & always close, embarrassingly close
no government and priest drowns it out entirely

what I hear now, the real mind,
the tongue inside your mouth.

## III.

Too many people listening
to get anything said

anything right.
Who hears, gets hurt.

Music freighted with such joy
as envenoms social forms,
quick run on the right hand
detoxifies the heart.
Wait. I've gotten beyond myself

or there is no self to get beyond.
There it is again, quickness saves,
the sperm is speed, accelerate
the happen, happiness,

a quick march for the King of Redonda        *M.P. Shiel*
who said in his long slow books
the best of all things is speed,
speed in the star the lights the eugenic night.

# 3. K.40

They're ready for me now
I want to be pretty in their sight

mew mew

eye eye
look at who

I'm me,
eye eye from

me at thee

at them the pretty
ones in smelly

taffeta how long
we've worn

these costumes
just to be born!

Eel pie on the long tables
marzipan and croque monsieur
pissaladière from Cavaillon
where sweetest melons grow

I have traveled all this world
to find myself in you

with you I mean your snuffy waistcoats
your powdery satin
can this be love, this mysterious
*glance* chains you to me?

And I feel nothing but being being
pure rippling being

spilling out of the shadows you try
to wake up with so few candles

where something you fear
and I can't guess

is waiting you think
for you to undress

and crawl into bed
while I keep talking.

## II.

It still means thinking.
That's the word.
My schoolmaster squabble:
is it thinking, is it singing?

I can't help any
body choose
I'm only for the ride
along in the weird
word car
I know another
way of talking
the fingers tell

wake
beside me many mornings
and I'll disclose
*the shimmering smile of far-off cities*          Stefan George
but won't be sad—
sorrow's taste
and will not swallow
I will swim in that dark river
but seldom drown
down into this bright life—

that is my secret,
tears dry sooner than the night—
my song says I'm not sure what it means.

## III.

Hurry there with me,
church is over
the people all flood out

Jews and Gypsies in the marketplace
keep stalls open for the Christians—
be grateful for black plums for crisp rolls
their iffy chicken salad, chocolates
smuggled over national frontiers.

These people love us with things!
While we were loving god with second-hand words.

# 4. K.41

Where have I been
the rain so here

sheet of glass
I break it with

eye fingers
break by seeing

through: then the tallest woman comes
to answer me and she
also has a weather she brings
from all the cat-infested prairies
where such leaves fall

Look – the egg has fallen from the tree
look – the shell was blue
look – the rain is on my hand
      and spots my pale blue shirt dark where it falls
look – water that dissolves all things
      gives stone its true color
look – we are fish down there
look – men still have to carry our genitals outside
look – we carry each other inside one another—

is that worth singing home about?

## II.

I see your signal on the hillside
you're waving at me I am guided

Where does going go?

A melody, then an amber person comes
and varies it a little
then we're almost done.

The rest is leaves
seafoam I mean
restless in wind
chittering the changes out
and all the while you wave to me
come across the lawn
eager as used to

but there is no am
no lawn only woods
no wood only hill
and the hill is far away by foot

I think it's you
it may be crow
or break a branch

spent so many years
traveling towards a broken tree

that speaks to me

not just at night, I wake
to see it at the edge or end
of seeing, a small dark gesture

beyond cheap commerce of affect signifiers.

## III.

Hurry sometimes is the only answer.

"Fear turns into desire" says Dante
speaking of the battalion of the newly dead
idling upon Acheron. Hurry over.
Hurry through your dread, your tired
endlessly repeated deed,
you can get through anything
Paschendaele or Plain of Jars
hurry with chains around your ankles
Siberian cathedrals beech groves of Mecklenburg maybe
a wild bull charging through the trees

he knows how to get there but stops and looks around
looks at you you look at him
the birds are singing and finally everything doesn't listen.

## 5. K.175

An army of it.

Army does it.
Day soldiers
filter through
pictures of trees
pines to me

and only me

My shadow is my fortress

up the ravelin
it all is war.
Polemos that extremity
the gods' amusement
when love gets out of hand
a steel band round the brows
filleting bluefish on the pier
an army is a navy though
a ship is just another knife

antlers. Horns
of the trees. Italies
full of them, tall
hurrying to sea.

But this is the strangest war
without bleeding
it's trying to teach something,
war is explanation

greed bleed
where's money
what does green
mean to a tree

*give me more mother*
the soldier cries, give me
the little box every shadow carries
snug in the heart of its absence—

is murder the only way to come home?

Busy trees today
making tomorrow
scattered corporals
chivvying recruits

excuse me, be bleeding

now after all it all
sorefooted limping from
mysterious battle—
that's just a guess reading
peculiar evidence in dead leaves.

## II.

A fountain.
Grace.
Shadow
bends to drink.

My shadow.
What can we do
with those who
do not want to learn?

What can we do with those who do not want to want?

Today hunters
stalking trees

baroque embellishments
of camouflage

outbursts of gun
at outbursts of geese

the sky's plain fact
will never wake us up

my shadow's thirsty
it is dry work being

dry sleeping so long
dry trying to remember

in sleep all the songs,
graceful shadow bend

low to remember
then step with me beside

the fountain when you bend
is shadows or reflections too

as if you drank
miracles of structure alone

evidence of you were
when you first heard the song.

## III.

a bird though
cries above it all
and the war changes

war wax
general rubble
ambulances on parade

pomegranates toppling
from a market stall
Chinese apples

we called them in that war
the only fruit where you
could taste the color itself

is that what I was following
through the woods around my house
color alone, animalless,

as if there were a place
to have come from
or a place to be here inside

and there never is,
morning is full of suppositions
a girl putting into her lips

a chunk of doughnut
stale before yesterday even
knows how to taste it new.

## 6. K.238

Nothing out there relaxes
so we have to.
The squirrel is tense, the crow
a-twitch with vigilance.
Idleness is ours
alone to explicate,

propagate. It is our job.
Or vigilante. We call it air
and all our young lives are spent
in fruits of idleness all round,
images ideas rhymes tunes tones

the apples of Sodom
stones. It's hard work to be easy,
we are building all day long
the structures of heaven,
bamboo scaffolding, girders welded

eyebeams overhead, lost sky,
painting a woman's breast to fit
inside a dome that's not there yet,
so hard to be easy, all about running,
running away and working peace,

running away from each other, dogs,
squirrels, so many variations
and no center, no medicine,
until someone makes a blue picture
persuades you to lie down and be still,

be touched.
Lie there, darling,
let morning lull.
This is the day
religion begins again

in a drowsy world
so hard to make sleep

so many gods used up
on the busy little road to now.

In the last age of the world
at last a science of touch.

## II.

O shepherd lend me one of your sheep
and one of your little Welsh dogs to guard her
shepherd lend me your flute so I can call
the valley from the hill and have them send
some maiden up to bring me lunch
a little cheese a little bread an apple
shepherd lend me your shaggy cloak
made out of last year's ram o shepherd
lend me your ears and tell me the time
how to make the flute make sense the tune
I warble never makes them dance shepherd
good shepherd lend me your soul so I can see
down the flowering hillside and teach myself
the names of what I see your map shepherd
lend me your map and let me go with dog and

flute and sheep and stumble, shepherd
lend me your staff so I don't fall down the rock
so I can have a measure of control over all
the animal potencies I have borrowed from you
shepherd lend me everything I need I will go
to the country they lead me to where everybody
knows everything and I can finally speak.

## III.

Blue flutter. Pages
of no book. Rhapsode
dithering with Homer's
heroes. Hollyhocks
speak Greek:
the king
is with his admirers
listening, they're strolling
in his garden far from the sea.

They scheme insurgency,
campaigns against the paynim
d'Outremer, armadas,
manifestos, new schools of art,
juntas, Anschluss, coups
d'état.
What else have men
to talk about?
Their will
has banished them
from any natural world—
they have run out of beasts to prey on,
appetites huger even than the garden,

they're hungry enough to eat a rose.
"One step at a time, Majesty,
our enemies are only shadows
but like shadows they are everywhere,
Majesty, around us and beneath us
and no step we can take leaves them behind."
"Your caution, Admiral, does you credit—
but have you never seen a shadow
swallowed up by the weary raptures of the sea,
a wave rises up in light and falls in dark?
Sail into the unbounded and bombard it—
then sail back to me and tell me
where your shells fell, and what strange
cities they laid waste unseen."

## 8. K.246 "Lützow"

Straw. We always are.
We always see
flowers in winter
made, colored with color
by a will to see.

I speak this language too,
am only an afterthought of it,

lyric footnote
to what everybody else said

a girl dancing by himself
a bird frowning at the sea

that proves nothing
just as touching you
proves nothing but that I have hands

But why do I always hurry, feel hurried,
why is such a quick animal
hunting all through me for the next thing to do?
Is it prey, cheetah, or the moon
you're after, little wolf?

The hard thing to remember is
next time be born in the same year—

tourists grin on the cathedral steps
their cameras, digital, are smaller now,

such childlike pleasures, I don't mind so much
the delicate jabber of English and Japanese

I have my own shadows to herd along the dusty road
my own language I'm trying to forget

the sun a cellphone ringing in my eyes.

## II.

Or not see so much:
a box, a box he brought in
to show us, empty,

"my mouth a disconnect," he said,
"if I can get the next trick new
I think the war will end"

but I'm not sure his kind of war
has even begun, not yet at least,
I sympathize with his mistake,

I took my skin for a flag once,
I imagined that what I felt was good for you
and you needed news of it

pronto and I did. Now he
feels that way too but without the feeling.
Brings the community a box.

A box is to put things in.
Things you don't have and maybe don't even want.
But those things also need a box to call their own.

Is there a war we really need?
Is there a circle with a cube inside it
a pair of dice with no spots
a man carrying nothing in his hands but
thinking or supposing the space between them
is a box, or space enough, gift, a man can carry

space with him wherever he goes?

## III.

A.
I know you now.

B.
This same road, a year ago.

A.
I know.

B.
You weren't sure about me then.

A.
And now.

B.
And now not either or not yet?

A.
I think I do, I think we'll go along the road a bit.

B.
Just as we did.

A.
It's strange to think that two people could walk along
a road and finally reach some city.

B.
It is strange. But why is it strange?

A.
The blossoms, some pink, some white in the chestnut trees where the little river hits the lake?

B.
Or their shadows. Why do we walk in shadow?

A.
Why are we walking at all? Didn't we once have the convenience of conveyance, wheeled?

B.
Wheels don't work anymore.

A.
Wind, there's wind.

B.
Always, on this road there's always wind.

A.
You see to know much more about this than I do. Have you been this way many times before?

B.
[Hums.]

A.
Am I supposed to recognize that tune?

B.
I don't know about 'supposed.' I sang it to you last time. It's the only one we know.

## 9. K.271 "Jeunehomme"

The things the things
the things one knows
and every tune is stored
and every new thing comes home

your father's shadow
on your mother's door

The Things
live in a world
a world is signs
an omen is the world talking about itself
and afraid, a sign
is a thing thinking about itself

the things know how to sing
the things know how to dance in dreams
the things are elsewhere when we wake

but the things are where we are
they are the angels

a thing is an angel

we move among them while they stand.

Thoughts embody'd
here on this empty road
a man is walking the familiar
the straight lines of his childhood
to taste the shadow of where he's been

## LISTENING THROUGH

To breathe things in
and make them breathe

the things that are his silent guardians
they keep watch
he feels them in his tears
when the sight of a cracked plate
or a crisp brown paper bag
not yet unfolded by the grocer
can make him full with feeling
he can't find any label for,
not joy not grief, a strange
intensity of now,

a thing
is always now

and when you've lost a thing
(I've lost my golden ring)
you've lost your now

Nowless then go sing
anytime you like

a lost boy on a lost road
looking for a lost thing

he'll never find
because a thing is now
and only here.

Saint Seraphim of Sarov
kept his monks and nuns apart
so each could seek the lostness of the other
and find and find,

patron of those who seek lost things
(I found my ring)
Saint Seraphim pray for him
this little boy this little me

I will throw all my other things away
and watch where they fall
then follow as well as I can
into the wilderness they show
by vanishing, and I will go there
and by losing I will know
where all the lost things go.

## II.

River that comes over the hill as mist
river that runs me, river of no remember,
all that is known about you is your passing,

no hint of where you're from or where to go,
river that is just an animal of passing,
slow as the sun, slow even as the darkness

river we are seldom permitted to see
but sometimes stand on the mulchy shore
watching driftwood, geese wild or resident,

the puzzling transactions of objects being moved
by something that looks like a republic of intentions
but no one I can stop and talk to, but you,

the whole of you, endure the flab of my address
all of us, brimming over with our ideas,
our ontologic jabber, river, listen one more time to me

river who swept Kant away along the shallow sea
river whose main cargo is the summer stars
meek reflections of the uneasy mind,

Tu Fu's river, river of pine green ornaments
that all are water, that all run through the hands,
river it is dangerous to understand

but I'm trying, living beside you year after year,
we live among signs and portents, we dream
only what the river brings to mind,

the actual water, the water that is you.

## III.

The steeple is falling
the street is full
this color bird
flies through the ground

the beggars run down the street
sailors carry flower girls around
it's all the way it was in books
when you could read.

No help for the drowning man
but go deeper.
No help for the hand
but to touch more.

Gold coins roll out of roses

frightened children hate the sound of words
a word is only to tell them what to do

run away, the light
is disobedient, it shows
more than it's supposed, the line
runs through the town, the circus horses
prance along the railway track
only the children are afraid.
Always afraid:

run faster. Stop and take a breath.
Go through your pockets. Raisins.
Dates. Stones. Enough to go on,
the forest is close now, frost comes soon,
people live inside everything,
people nobody has ever seen,

there is always somewhere else,
there isn't always only here,

only the dried fruit in your pocket
the little stones to keep you company
take them out and name them
and they will be your little soldiers
but even they keep telling you what to do.

To be is to be told.

Sometimes you sing, sometimes you get
so angry you don't even want to breathe.

You want to disobey, just disobey,
then you look at the stone again
and it still tells you freedom comes from doing
whatever it says. Freedom is being here.

## LISTENING THROUGH

You don't believe a word of it, all you want
is to get away, away and never listen. Then
break free, run fast, and learn to disobey
this palpitating Torah of the heart.

## 11. K.413

Hold a curl. A curve.
Over the room is room around me.
Roof. A word?

A word is a knife with no bread.

Push harder at the missing door.
Milk. She's always

on time I'm always late

trip the marble steps
weather means danger

carved hillside
images in rock
image is the only treasure

pictures are huge rooms
each one a different shape

a telling

each one empty

a treasure is something waiting for you
you have to plug yourself into its sense of space
to seize the treasure and sail home

sail, veil, no home, no treasure
but the empty rooms
each room a different shape of big

shape is our treasure

you sashay past you empty me
each me a different you

shape? pleasure,
pronounced as in Oklahoma
one time in summerwind the wheat

first syllable rimes with play
the second measure

girls are running over the large but unpretentious lawn
to be on time
you are hurrying outward to them and through them
to be late,
pleasure!
something you forget,
pleasure! something somebody else
has to remind you of,
that is what somebody else is for,

*[cadenza:]*
Do I have to tell you again?
Up the ladder, gold-eyed
wood of the granary door
where the Dogon shield their millet
push open, crawl in,
call a name softly, there you are.

## II.

so long ago not so far away
we walked along Italian streets
never got around to our affairs
which must have been with the stars

then you sent a letter
with a picture
trolley car and snow
can such things be

when we never got around to business and all the stars
that push people around never looked the other way,
no chance, and I thought about you taking the Thalien-
strasse streetcar out to the end of the line then riding
back quietly getting ready for the middle of things

we always get ready for the middle because we both know
everything is getting further and further away all the
time and we are stars too evidently goodbye goodbye Big
Bang and all that babble about the infinite recedingness
of the universe everything departing everything rushing
everywhere and everywhere there is anyway is just away

away from me and not so long ago and the city not far,

Everything exists to keep people apart
who otherwise would fall into each other
and make a bed of everything

when everything is supposed to be
busy with its Father's business
carrying everything else so far away

and then I looked down
at the cold little stream runs past my house
and saw a little fish hurrying there too.

I miss you. But the French say
*you are missing from me.*
So when we meet some day
and ask who's to blame
let's hold hands and blame the little fishes.
Improper plural. *Tu me manques.* Blame words.

## III.

Flags fly under water

cobblers work frantic for the emperor
and everything changes.

This music is about everything that changes
and for once has something to say

about that most vexed agent
everybody. It says: beneath
the ocean another earth is waiting

beyond the sky another sky is breeding.
What we use up will be replaced
and somebody else will use us up—

how beautiful the wet banners of vanished kingdoms,
how beautiful a king is
when he is all power but has none,

when he rides in the tumbrel to the guillotine
or when a queen rules a continent she has never seen
army-less, and with her smile alone—

take back my words
from politics and money,

let it be that when I speak
beneath my word
another word is waiting

and when I breathe
another's breath is speaking.

## 12. K.414

In the middle of things
the hunt
methodical a kind
of joyous plod.

Hunt.
There is a king in your pocket
a moon on your back

and already it's dawn.
Who knows you?

*

Not what I see but that it makes me seen
or to have been seen, silently hailed,
two persons passing in and out of phase,
their shadows touch—

ancient marriage!

*

Tell me all
things lying in dead leaves
are full of life, is that

is that what you were getting at
in a year of your life

the hunters stolid through the woods
their white hounds distracted

readily by truffles, bitches
mostly, under the leaf mould, under
such oaks by which a stag once bled,

bratchet, such dogs are picked
to bark or bell in tune,

harmony animals
glisten of their teeth,

what are they after,
this posse, so quiet?

No bear no deer
and the trees stand close
marshaled it is no thrill
to gallop through

still they keep coming
could they be after me
and if they are or do
who is this me supposed to be?

*

I look down and count my legs
I look up and count the sun

timeless error to be me.

They're taking their time about it
but never stop
I pray to them but the trees suck up all sound

the king's out of my pocket now
running for his life

woodpecker, mountain stream, campfire ashes cold,
the hunters play cards till it's too dark to see.

## II.

Not so never here

hands cupped around your face
skull ears

you hear their skin

your lips move slowly
you followed the finger
pointing words out in a book

bright clean fingernail
shows breath where to go

pronounce this sentence

then try to remember it
the name of the one you need
is hidden inside it

the one you need to need
is inside the sound of what you see

I have given it all to you
her name her hawk
her tower her little yellow car

she who once in Anatolia
was mistress of such beasts
lives near you now
almost inside you

now it is squirrel only or flying
fox and bat because you
are only who you are at night

and here the sun comes over the summerhouse
he must have been the loneliest man who ever lived
so hard he had to work to say the simplest thing

it goes on without me

and with no you and no me
the shadows would still come crashing through the trees

## III.

it has no heart here
it locked it in a golden chest
in a tired garden

story books tell what giants do
smaller monsters like me and you

what happens inside the earth
and there too the giants hide their wits
where we hide our wants

come out come out
empty head with ruby rattling in it
word moving

and let the new religion come
sunbreak over little hill
we speak another language here

they are resplendent
in silken mistakes

heirloom vocabularies
lady I would be a word in your mouth
he said and no other commodity
be our community

came a phone call from the weather
just the sound of wind
breathing when you answer

just the sound of sun.

And at your backdoor you hear the cloud.

## 13. K.415

Stars do it.
You do it. Speeds
out from the middle to.

Here. Take this.
I have carried it so long
and from so far

so long so far so here
take this

it has no shape
and it has eyes in it

at first I thought you were the sky
then they started talking

some story the eyes got busy with
about two birds or a green box

who can tell the ins and outs of
what is color to a bird

but you eyes
have always seen me coming

the only tragedy: when a man has to say
I never had what I had

as if his life it had no shape
and his eyes were closed

## LISTENING THROUGH

two birds in no box
and they were blue

so far carried, fetched
the dream slipped jewels on my fingers

autist artist
and I couldn't keep the cat

and the cat ate the bird
there was no bird

a big yellow stone on his magic finger
and he told me who gave it to him

and and and

There is a ripple runs through all things
uneasy play someone's in the house
you think but never a girl just a voice

a voice with no eyes
and she looks at you
too much magic too little math

so I stripped off her pearls and gave them back to the sea
I hid the car keys from myself
and locked the tower door but it was too late

all the sound has come down the stairs
seeped into the room and formed a single word
thank God I don't know the language that it spoke.

## II.

Scull across the lake
put effort in it
get nowhere fast

I love the amplitude of noon
mommy when do the trees sleep
are we the only people who lie down

boaters floating away from their bad consciences
who was your father in the war
everyone has a murder or two to hide

some high finance with the petty cash
a twisted thing in the mousetrap still bleeding
unanswered mail unspoken mind

guilt is the same size as itself, same grade
losing anything is like losing everything
even the littlest

so don't let your pretty fingers trail
in the cool water alongside the canoe
who knows who's down there hungry

waiting to marry you and already
the twinkling wedding band
flashes in the sky coming for you

where we have been above and down below
and have been two there too
playing at being one

lie back and let me paddle
thunder at the end of afternoon
I like the little thing you sang to me—

*no more religion* – what tree said that
or did its shadow find you
and for once you simply understood?

## III.

Tamerlane, barking at his troops,
paused and remembered
a valley full of apricots

remembered he liked boys as well as girls
remembered he could not write his name
but ruled the world, remembered he was lame.

His soldiers were accustomed to his spleen,
his silences, they loved him the way only tyrants
can be loved, collecting such totalities of trust,

they waited and thought as little as they could
lest they be thinking the wrong think when he spoke again,
but he was waiting, he was tasting

apricots again and auburn weather,
and half a dozen little more than children
who met him once and one of them smiled,

a little girl in the hills above Trebizond
when all the rest were solemn and afraid,
and who am I, he thought, who could I be at whom

even a child presumes to smile?
There seemed no point in going on,
we do what we do to tame the world.

He left the parade ground and his soldiers knew
they had lost their king. A man
who remembers apricots is already too far away.

# 14. K.449

Suns come up hard here.
Interrupt
to leave a space
for you to hear.

Kiss my white collar
and I kiss your waist
where blouse leaves skirt
and shows we all know

*the shimmer of far-off smiling cities*
or whatever it was Stefan George said
moved me so much I moved it
into my martyrology my High Mass

the shabby marble mantelpiece
of my memory where it still rests
a little dusty maybe maybe changed
to make it more like the mind that holds it

the way we remember

Things change
untouched
they alter
or fingered by our
half-alert attention

Every time you remember something you wear it out

How long will we go on having the *Iliad*?

Smoother everything flows
till soft as cheese
it crumbles when you try to lift it
fresh to some intimate occasion yuck

stale as your feelings
felt again and again
always the same always yours

It stumbles along beside you
this body-of-feelings all-your-life
like a shadow you can smell.

\*

Hard sun. Vague wood.
Save me
from my answers.

Cross your hands here
you're a Christian or a Mason
trying to tell me something
but my eyes are closed

So you say it again

your hand

a word in the dark.

## II.

Under this river
there is a river
flows another way

LISTENING THROUGH

where quiet tribes
climb blue rocks

kiss me in Dutch
little animal

you who discovered
the *other way* of water

how nothing ever
can descend to us
unless some other rises

\*

Twist-lipped flower salmon and saffron
roses of winter commerce—
the flower salesman
tracks you to your lair
and lays his pretty samples
all round the cave mouth
and breathes the fragrance of them
inward where you cower

like me afraid of sunlight
especially the kind of light
that hides in flowers

the tiny rivers rafting
red through animals.

This kind of beauty I can withstand.
This kind of river? I have one of my own,
I keep it in a little bottle by the stove.

Advertising. Alembic. Currents
of what once were feeling. Yet another
river. Stream over stream
falling and never mixing, stream
under stream.

## III.

Sometimes aren't you me?
Tired too of dancing in the amber room?

I'm tired of ruling so many Russias
I just want to file my toenails
and watch the egrets fish my pond.

Everything is mine. And I am you,
make free with yourself,
I am all permission. I am yours.

Body. Bowl. The Deep Drink
a wizard brewed in her cauldron
to tell me about you.
Why ask her,
drugs need us
so we can release into sound
all their dubious gospels
into a world desperate to believe
anything as long as it has no name.

Poetry is this idiot
who uses language

to find out what lives
on the other side of names.

Who climbs the mountain that is not there.
I have washed the ocean till we both are clean.

## 15. K.450

My horn my horn is a habit
a little forest to know you in

\*

where a star fell
a stag died

a spurt of his life-stuff
grows mushrooms there

truffles deep
in the growl of ground

no one found
not even the white sow

Aeneas spotted snoring on the bank

Woods woods fingers
erasers
more erasers than pencils
more lines than squares
toadstools and tomorrow
more and more

volume of a frustrum
(amputated cone)
examine, heap up formulas.

More formulas than things!

Sweaters for morning
a shawl for night time

a shawl with stars
woven into it

try to tell the pashmina from the air
around it not easy

as near as I can figure
you never were an island—

I saw that tree
moving through those trees

*Codex Seraphinianus*
lovely fake who needs a flower
when we have an hour
who needs a little cat
when we have symmetry?

We're all a little autistic you know,
John especially, and we are all named John

(as the poet wrote), what else would you name
a tree come walking up the road and

we don't need even pictures of them
we have words
we don't even need words
we have this funny feeling in our heads
the great land between our ears
from sea drone to sly sunset
so many cities
and god is word enough for *we*

a god is a word the mind says to me.

Quite impressive. Now listen to this:

teapot broke
tea ran south
a river comes
a river knows
the tea is me
the sea is close
we drown
among ancestors
we do not know,
we orient ourselves
by how we smell

and I smell the night again
coming over the hill.

## II.

Let it think nothing while I try
also to be a table
gloss of a grey morning
removing one by one
such thoughts as pretend they think.

Arriving, arising.
A method to each wave.

I know these numbers, officer,
they have counted me before,

I know the feel of each of them,
this seven pressed against my skin.

And the one thing no one can forgive is love.

O you sly song
you stone hidden in brown leaves
you last meaning left in the world.

Tree. Tree. So many me.

How can I ever be slow as you need be?
Hyperactive disorder
boy in the cellar
chasing silverfish down the whitewashed wall.

Inside every brick
a letter from the fire

he is too busy to hear
though he rests his head against the cool wall.

## III.

Everyone is here now
I can stop being.

It's all about them and me.
This is the you I used to be.

The one I knew, her father
was a baker, she sat in the flour
like a curved white song,

her father was a blacksmith
she learned from him
how to bend me round her finger

*nagelneu,* brand new, shiny
new nail

hammering the guesswork quick together
to make it stand,

her father was a carpenter
and taught me how to build a tree
late afternoons when I sat in his atelier
waiting for her to finish titivating and come down

then we'd go walking out together
strolling through the forest her dad had made

When we got to the oil well in the middle
I always forgot what kind of oil it was
It changes every day she said
sometimes oil of mountain sometimes oil of sea

Is it good for us I asked
so many times
Try it and see she said
night after night holding close
but never did but never did
even now I taste it on her skin

no, you never licked me
no, the oil stays in the well
the way the wood stays in the tree

no one gets married any more
and a rusty nail is pretty too

a red kind of remembering,
a girl in fact with no father at all.

# 16. K.451

Her voice is the same as his voice
said the tree I feel in my limbs
my body crawls with information and

Just and. All the rest
is things trying to sing, matter
trying to mean.

Hylomorphic symmetry,
things trying to make sense
perfect but alive
the way a whole sky fits into a lake.

More. The ripple
runs through you,
not the spine
that common highway
but through the subtle
strange and devious
pathways,
meat is made of undergrowth
sly asides, massacres and touch,

trust, that's where the signal runs,
politics *is* physiology,
look at any Vatican
and feel inside your skin
the organ tones of someone's business,
selling the clouds, buying your time
with the smell of roses,

Christ what a mystery
it is to be alive at all.

& then, my gorgeous little ampersand
with your cute bottom you
impersonate the next obligation in my job
and we agree to call it love, love,
since what else is there to talk about

it all comes back
to the simple minute underneath the tree
when you and what you see
suddenly seem to be two

can't blame that on the snake
and the sky swells out above the lake
and nothing fits any more,
sobbing gentlemen sit in shadow
scratching their stubble and write the bible

there has to be a record of these early days
when dualistic –hence impure– vision first arose
when everything went on inside
and only later spilled, slopped
over the rim of the cup

the way the sky (I'm sorry
to keep boring you with that blue tune)
slips out of the lake at last and runs away

night, stars, mist, and we
call this behavior a child

'not paying attention'
and slap him once or twice
not too hard the way
the branches slap against
each other in wind
a slip or slap here or there
and he really doesn't mind
do you?

## II.

Fuse my shadow to your body—
that's all the alphabet
is ever asking,
like the Spanish Main,
seductions, Carib vistas,
driveways paved with shells
crushed white Atlantic
sunlight
all those lives
crunch under my feet
and you blame me, calling
me your desert island.
But I am amber. Build
your house of me.

Name more silly little countries,
I have to struggle against your tenderness,
that dinner made up of nothing but dessert.

But there is an idle island where it is bare
where birds are the secretaries of the sky
and scribble nonsense on the sand
while they scream into their airy phones

on an eternal lunch break, shadows,
and we walk among their doodles, shadows
ever changing, but our business, duty even,
is to make sense of it, become
rabbis of it, lowly members of their parliament

Just let it someday get so quiet
the mind is forced to listen to itself
and leave the girls alone.

## III.

The root is in you, you are folk,
the whole folk, the lore,
the time at sea, harvest
and lost property, umbrella upright

shoved in a rice field, train
and truckle bed, lascivious clergymen
and an old red bull leaning on the rain,
be reasonable for once, you can't

get away from where I am.
For many make me.
Every kiss a thousand marriages.
It has to mean something, it keeps moving.

It nears us of each other, you mean me,
we are the marriage bed of primitive vocabulary
we are the pebble in the flour
sift, sift, till we are sifted

till death comes hobbling towards me
and because I am so many

## LISTENING THROUGH

I run away in every direction
and outwit his compassionate fumbling

bone fingers on my rusty door
he forgives me every time.

## 17. K. 453

How can I hear you
when I know your name

things too close
appear to be on fire

they walk around like mirrors
you want to take a mallet to them

but when one thing breaks
everything breaks

a hand is the slyest wind

\*

"the things we think we see or mean"
it said in my dream and so I said it too

a leaf is when no one listens
sky is when someone is gone

The children break their mirror
now each one has her own

the closer you get to the mirror
the more you leave out

seeds fall out of the sun
sun stands in the sky where it rises in winter

when there are enough contradictions
men fall in love with women

I cannot say how the reverse of this may occur,
the only time I ever was a sky it was night

a clear night in January
and all I could see were the unknown lights in me
that kept us both warm,
forgot to look at myself in the looking glass

but maybe night has no mirror
just the brittle names of heaven.

\*

The irritating thing about a flute
is a flute always sounds like somebody loving you
and you don't know who it is
and you're not sure you want their affection
let alone the intimacy their sound proposes

so you run to the doorway
and keep opening and slamming the door
and everything is still there outside
only for once you have said what you wanted to say.

## II.

There are no defenders here, no battlements—
all my life I've spent
besieging a deserted city.

A page of wheat,
black waves
history is only habits.

There is a word
that spoke itself
and wise women sit around and listen

teach their sons and daughters
go out and measure it
and while you're at it
go measure where the shadow falls

then break something
and cry your way home
holding the pieces before you
and the tune of your sobbing
is all we'll ever know
of what you found and how long
it was or deep or color,
did it have color, or was it
something on the other side of seeing?

## III.

No life is wasted
but everybody could have done more.

Drink this song then go to sleep,
wake up to know
you just missed something the sun said.

Wielding white and black paint such
as to suggest color where they meet, *Juan Gris*
color from no color born,

color is contradiction.
Gold on my finger warms my knucklebones,
all I am is what I feel.

The world never seems bigger
than the culture we see it from
then we go up in a plane and size is born,

the size of what you want
is always smaller than what there is,
and that's where love comes in

like the Austrian cavalry
bright-tunic'd through beech trees
hunting you down,

feel me or die,
feel me, no matter how fast you run
the shadow of my sound will get there before you

and you will sink down exhausted
into the being I make you feel
even if you never feel me

it is the contract with the earth you signed.

## 18. K.456

Ice rime frost *canities*
hunting weather
to where it rises

everything comes out of the woods.
Carl Ortwin Sauer disagrees,
everyone comes from the shore—
we are littoral:
from coast moved inland
only where river let us, led us.

*Aeneid* shows the pattern,
Book VIII, upriver, ascend.
Into the ever woods. The woods

are where we're bound
to be born. The white
sow and the brown boar.

Incest. We lied, we said we were wolves.

And so the morning was.

All this waking up, noble
touching,
caring one another,

so much such.
So much it hasn't started
yet the familiar

## LISTENING THROUGH

silences. The familiar silences.
Now you know Bernini's aesthetic
the bronze church and the marble ship,

you know the sunshine
carved out of oak wood,
dangerous polished stairs

stars in every window
as if it were always night.
Or Santa Maria della Salute

as if nighttime never came.
Bloch's Berlin. Sauer's Berkeley.
The long streets. Nothing holds us.

Only the *sentence* leads us to one another,
the distances, unspoken, the blue flash
from the welder's torch, carved pineapple,

learn this dead language, darlings,
stand up tall and learn your opera.
This is my last gospel: turn

everything into some sort of kiss.
Now I'm lost. I couldn't have meant
something as simple as that,

could I, a crow on the lawn,
perhaps I did. Let me count my fingers,
fit them to all the keys,

keyholes, shinny up the flagpoles,
get stuck in the sky, never come down,
a lesser number, something between 2 and 1,

dim in midday, still give a little light
come dusk, when the herdsman stumbles
over the bull skull by the gorse bush and groans.

## II.

Around, um, around,
arm around, um, I'm hard to see,
arm around arm around tumble from
woods in ground mist risen, a bell
jingles as if one of the dead before me
were getting a phone call down there,
I can almost speak the sad words
the little song proposes to the mind,

absurd sincerity of a machine
I see the dead soldiers
stumbling through the woods
Ambrose Bierce's story
the child sees only the aftermath
men with bleeding feet
lost in the trees. I try to think,

try to think of something else
but everything turns into war.
It is Christmas morning, even the music
permits it, in the book it says
When the whole world was at peace
at Bethlehem in Judaea the Christ was born,
But the name of the book is Martyrology
and he will never be born again.

LISTENING THROUGH

The cellphone rings, or the Carolina wren
suddenly back or not yet gone
winters with us and has something to say
recognizable, appearances around us
are still comprehensible, i.e., permit
sentences to composed about them
the mad mind of the listener somehow
makes cohere. Only fear
makes us believe, Spinoza said
And fear aborts valid inference.
No church too dumb to say your prayers.

## III.

Doesn't have to be anything
just has to be.

No argument,
serenity.

Swallowing reflex disturbed
in certain neurological conditions.

Circular reasoning. In war
poinsettia. Named

after someone. Candle, canticle,
Africa named for sunshine

like the apricot cooked by the sun.
In schoolyards the little boy

kicked and punched continues
to die. Big surprise.

Where do I go now
now that I have lost the shadows

you entrusted to my care
and where

with sun always in my eyes
and midnight always an accusation

I can claim *My father
did this to me*

but look what I did to my father,
I was and I am and I am

look at the insistence with which I insist
I am no one and nowhere and don't listen to me

do you hear me, stop listening,
all I ever meant was music

and you have that already
look down in your lap

from the heights of where we always are
climbing breathless up a level plain.

# 19. K.459

Swim swimming. [*orchestra*]
Accuse the thing
of being

being what I want
or not
it to be.
Swim. A leaf
as acanthus or
some spiny
sunburnt
fate a leaf
in plaster
to mark your wall
a part of nature.

You are you
because swim.
Things swim.
Wind swims your backyard.

The child comes out to play. [*piano enters*]
It has played this game
before. It may be he is born
knowing how to play.
To move each bead in place
or swim the air. The prodigy.
It may be weather
that teaches him though,
does he listen deeply
enough to the weather,

watching the clouds
yield to sun the sun
to clouds and both to night.
He watches all day long.
Then follows the sun
home, goes in, he is home,
all through winter evenings
he remembers the game.
The molecules of it.
With a coal on the hearthstone
he tries to draw the game,
makes marks. Marks mean
he thinks. A clock
looks down from the mantle
in the shape of a cat, it
is no part of his game.
A statue of a saint beside it
but he never remembers
her name. Bare feet. The moon.
When his mother comes to look at the marks he's made
on the stone he has to distract her. This is not for her to
see. Don't give anything away. Mother, why do we wear
clothes, he asks, Mother, why do we eat three times every day? Mother would you sew a button on my coat, an
ivory button maybe or a button made of horn?

Bone. Horn. Baby,
where do ideas come from,
why are your fingers black
why does every child I have lie to me?
What do these marks mean?

*

Moth and mildew,
milk and money
mother mind,
horn and bone
your only child

mother baby
silver tooth
baby mother
untell truth

o mother I am going fast
faster than forest

o baby you are staying just as you are
it is the sunshine that is going
and I will never tell you how far

O mother mother I already know.

## II.

Suppose rose.

Yellow.

Wind sin
color enough.

Touch till
never. Stone
among stone
radical *why*.

An initial carved on a coping
or gouged there, easy
letters to incise, I's,
all our names begin with I.
Pick a number at random.
Then apply it to ladybugs
and see them crawling up a white stone
then count the dark little spots
on their cinnabar or sandarac shells or wings.

Think. The mind thinking
is a kindly surgery,
the blood and lymph that flow
are poetry and prose.

There, that's a comparison complete,
expressed in the simple colors of the absolute.

Meet me at the roadhouse in 1943
how can you forgive me for the war?
I drive there through the fluttering leaves
in a '38 LaSalle. You wait in satin.
We lose our third dimension as we flirt,
shadows we eat, I light up a resemblance,
on shadows we get a little drunk
and linger in the flickering moonlight motel.

## III.

So to become a cliché
is better than thinking one,
yes easier to climb out
of the black and white frames
back into the world of color
which wins us with tricks of its own.

## LISTENING THROUGH

Coleridge, *Biographia litteraria* chapter 13.
That's what we need, an arrogant obvious,
a mode that means
invention absolute,
but we can say anything
only because it's all been said before

other islands other dictionaries
other woman with long hair in her eyes.

Distinctions. I can think
because I speak. Silent,
what thinks in me
is only colors,
colors and contours
touching each other,
changing shape, moving
away, never a word,

thinking without words
is only colors, leaning
on things or leaving things
potent in the smallest
sky that still surrounds the mind.

I hear you (I think it means)
only because I hear me first

Like an animal I am,
holding words in my teeth,
as I run towards you
then in my excitement roaring out
and letting them fall, bite,
fasten the idea of my mouth on the idea of your thigh.

## 20. K.466

hudor root of water
water, know you
you make apple

there is nothing yet anywhere but an apple on the tree

in silvery clothes a woman waiting

meals ago a glass
there is nothing yet but a glass
the glass is waiting

waiting is empty

things do our deeds for us if we rest

water does it

it is a little like morning a little like lime

your eyes close together
what makes it cohere
and still be free

why can't we who are mostly water
behave with that coherent liberty?

but is water free?

But outside Cooper Union
in the great triangular they call a square

## LISTENING THROUGH

twenty thousand waited
indifferent to the debaters'
practiced insincerities within,
palaver unending, just like war,
but the crowd waited, knowing only
they would be martyred by the outcome

all a crowd ever does is wait
the outcome is built into the stars
of how we are
the preacher shouted
in the cold, the only cure
for slavery is for all men to be slaves

white and black and in between
all slaves, and only their masters free
those strange thick men who smell of verbena
and whose skins are the color of money in moonlight

For we are only water
one woman thought
and always find our level
fill every cranny
touch everything and leave
everything we touch
soaked with ourselves

glistening comely clean
glass amber stone china
glistening clean clear
knives spoons fingernails
a summer's face come
smiling up on Coney sands
pretty comely amatory

loose lonely o my new
born child come
dripping with my
waters too and then

it dries. And then it dries.

## II.

Can I hear you yet?                                *for N. M.*
Dear so like dead or like
deaf, your small blue car
across what slapping highway
pelts, do you even remember
that there is something to remember?

This morning I need to know something about dying
so I turn to you, I loved you when you were young
and never knew it, there was a line
around you and a still awareness
that wasn't aware of me, hardly even of you,
I loved the clean limbs of your ignorance
about yourself, you were the society

you were born, water in clear water
poured, and you were decent, pretty, smart.
So I turn to you, now that you've had
a dozen years to be social with the dead,
tell me, is the company there like here,
must I be to that manner born
to do death decently?
Can I hear you hearing me this morning
mildest December, the hills of your Brewster

still autumn green, red-tailed hawks frequent,
vultures up here too, and eagles,
and still the conscientious crows patrol,

you have left me this whole mild
protestant word to take care of for you
and I'm not even sure I can hear you
hearing me this morning, can't ask you to speak,
you let me speak at last, to tell you
how the silent liberty of all your constraints
spoke long legs, fingers, your shy green eyes.

## III.

Old sky scrapers
when nouveau
still was new.
They looked like
fountain pens
standing on end.
What did they write
in the sky, guns
aimed at God?

I think of little clerks
in starched white shirts
my father at his desk
with glinty spectacles
or trotting up and down
so many stairs for
exercise between
the sound of money and
what else can he hear?

How old a city is so fast.
A man lasts longer
than a sentence
or a stadium, a high
house, office tower.
Nothing lasts longer than me.
The transplanted
rhododendron still
lives outside the kitchen,
shivers in mild wind.
For instance.

The army invests the deserted city,
puzzled soldiers press buttons
elevator doors open and close.
They ride up and down all day,
hone their spears on marble stairs,
what was the purpose of all this
they wonder. And suspect at last
that those who built it
had no idea themselves.

# 21. K.467

Far quiet
to hear
the hum behind the head

"do you think it was there,
the forest, pond,
before you woke?"

"it was round,
the sun shone in,
things already
and knew what to do"

listen to them – it could never
be otherwise, a month
with no eight in it, a tree
reflected in the lagoon, the canoe
slices right through the reflection

"film that in turn, level
upon level, even further
from the real
deep into what you feel"

but the other doesn't answer
locked in contemplation
of the mysterious lagoon,

its whence. Its hither.
People just want to know.

"Some people."
"And the others?"
"Speak another language,
 one without nouns.
A number system
without eight."
"Why eight?"
"Oh pick a number,
 divide it by me…"

they're smiling at
each other now
drift out of earshot
a shape on water.
Canoe.

\*

When you're washing dishes
and come close to the end
suds thick at the bottom of the emptying sink
you see strange writing in the foam
you trail your finger through it
to write more, you write your father's name.
It even lasts a few seconds
before it dissolves into everything
you ever thought before.

Dyslexia. Royal throne rooms.
Satin jackanapes prancing,
ladies in fancy waiting, coiffures
like Babylon, a woman
and a man either side
of their retarded son
refusing to admit anything

wrong with their fine young man.
Dancers. The music
of denial. A few are drunk.
After all that's what music's for,
majesty asleep, love climbing
up the espalier, the skin
on love's hands smell like pears
(a picture of you smelling it).

## II.

Water when we leave it alone.
Pond at dawn. Midday lagoon.
Even frost on the green hill,
so simply the many things
and water always only one.

Water when we remember,
old man carrying a red brick,
old woman without a coat,
a cat walking nowhere,
the secret fuel of everything we love

animates the world around us,
engine of the immediate hums,
the secret fuel of every decent action
washes the stone steps of your house,
Baltimore morning, rivers
through your dreams, little brook,

little wooden bridges, o water when it
loves you interferes with schemes
of edifice and ownership, only winter
knows how to tie water down
and God has taken all our winters away.

## III.

The diamond cracks.
Planes of cleavage
each one a Midnight Mass

pray in your sleep
sip the golden cup

Crystals have catastrophe built in,
each particular to itself
the lines where fate comes in,
the lines of me.

Through long years of mastery
I grew a crystal somewhere deep.
Doctors called it a disease
but I knew better – this hard
knot was the me of me,

loud at times, with a merry
feeling reaching down my arms
as if I were dancing with somebody fine
and what my hands felt
ran back up my arms
and stored that information
in the augmenting crystal,

sunlight fed it and the dark
gave it milk,
everything I ever saw
seems to be reflected in it

facet by facet, playful stone,
fatal luminescence of the sayable—
because finally I called the crystal by my name.

## 22. K.482

Dragon is a dragon still.
Smoke of Danube
caverns. Duna. Passed
once over the Iron Gates
as if I were a piece of air
safe from everything
but breath. But some
being was breathing.
Breathing a word.

A man with a cobbler's awl
conducts an orchestra of mice.
And this is Germany again
*langue* I loved and land amazed.

Astonished land
turned to stone
pine log outside Lauterbach
fresh cut, red inner bark
fragrant, vapor rising
from morning dew.

Dragon has to be.
Smoke in Leipzig
a tall tree of poinsettias
in Wiesbaden,
at the baccarat
and no wheel for him,
our only heaven
the hands of other men.

*Nos autem homines*
and what else were we
to begin, every Catholic
knew a piece of God
back then, put them all
together and could fit in the mouth,
Lord's Latin—

the dragon said:
all that's just a piece of air,

sweet air, called *aria* in opera,
called gasp in the hospital room
where my mother couldn't catch hers,
her breath kept trying to go out,
go forth and be gone, quiet quiet
her breath, soft little gasps,
as if she knew not to fight too hard
to keep what by its nature is always leaving,

sweet air, and then no more breathing,
and the selfish air goes out to fill
all the rampant selves in sunlight still,

so many I have seen die
once is enough
the dragon said
to teach you what to do

and where you travel
following the breath
to where it goes.

And who is this dragon,
the power of anyone who breathes,
pounds the piano, speaks the oboe,
orders his men to ready their rifles,
aim, and Maximilian falls.

The watch unwinds then
and I can feel no more
and I too fall, the way a body falls.

## II.

Acanthus leaf
or something like,
stiff and spiny
sculpturous
is that a word,
Eve, my artist,

sculptress, how's that,
for a sad old genome

cloning into the west?
Where love is, that

dramatic difference
you have taught men

to carve out of the wood of war,
biology of plants and men,

neurosis of glaciers and rivers,
Eve, how can we sit

so close together
only a million years

apart and still
see your clear eyes?

in the day of music
I hear no religion.

*

One is a rough agate
tumbling in grit
to be polished
fine by friction
of attending

listen listen
all you have to do,
I do all the
work the music says

agate I was
and flute I am
and nothing forgets
no business to be me.

*

One by one the lovers speak
until Eve chooses
then up the wooden hill
to Bedfordshire
where my ancestor

beneath the quilt reads Sophocles
and waits and waits

in a world that wants to make every boy a girl
and every son become his dad's Antigone,
names, conditions, aspirations. Sophocles!

The arrant madness of knowing anything at all
like Kafka standing in the snow
midnight in a nameless town.

## III.

Unwearied caravan of I am
trekking across the manyness of sand.
What an endlessness of me,
disgusting gazetteers, autistic atlases,
mildewed maps I follow to keep on.
Dead general, no quartermaster to feed us
and still the infantry of me hobbles on,
the merchants we're escorting
lost their cargoes long ago,
the panniers of their camels are full
only of dust only of shadows,
cool dust sweet in this dry sand.
Someone is always humming, we follow
the tune by night, follow the color
by day and getting there becomes
a fabulous religion. No gods in these places.
At sunset we sing our dreary anthem
and rest an hour, trying to catch
between day and dark that one
interstitial gate a few of me feel
we were one day promised. But by whom?

And where could it lead
more commodious than this vastness,
could it be the gate of a walled city
in which Being found better employment
than just Going On? Sometimes
we listen so hard we think we hear
the squeak or groan of that gate spreading
open. Or it could be closing, who can tell?
Rusty screws tightening further the organs
of our perception, mind driven mad
by listening alone. Night march.

# 23. K. 488

It could be anybody's face
the smile
micro-managed muscles
saying

what we are supposed to see.

There is an embeddedness to things
how we wake with an image in mind,
risen then, risen to appear
from never know where.

Birdland. Boardwalk.
Dreamland. Ballroom. Cakewalk
before your father was born,

and you walk that way too
cradling colors in your arms,

you've got class, you carry
your smile like a basket of fruit
contadina, citizen of the tender cliché

all government bows to your power,
Pomona, radical,
let the bulls
fight each other a while and let men sleep.

Unless they wake dreaming of you
and the dream sticks to the corners of the room,
shadows, pale window frame

revealing nothing,
no clock anywhere.
No time to tell.

\*

And then he thinks of you again,
and this time you're talking,
all talk and no reaction
just the way he likes it

a swan with no sugar
a radio without a single flame
someday he will write down
a catalogue of all his father's silences,

their flavors and durations
then he'll come to yours
the unforgiven index of what you never said
and smiled all the while you never said it.

Then the day takes over.
We have longer obligations:
to mourn the murdered dictator
on our way to mourning those he killed

and made the likes of us complicit
paying our silent taxes for this war or the next
then quick as a bird flying away from the window—
suddenly I know what silence is for.

And what will I do with what I know?
Let it fall, dear friend, armload
of leaf and flower on the empty table.

## II.

Poinsettias. Red bract
big on someone else's
petals. Dull green leaves.
A quality of saturated color
but with no brightness,
no sheen. No shine.

It used to scare me,
still does a little, so red, so dead,
and the twenty foot tall tree of them
in Wiesbaden, can't get that out of my mind,
as if in every lifetime you
have to come to this bright casino
where colors lose their own sheen, shine,
and Dostoevsky flees by night
leaving thousands of rubles in bad debts,
one for every day of his life,
running from his life
through the ever increasing numbers,
numbers where the distances are stored
alone can heal him, hide him
from what he wants to be.

And I have walked with him
from the casino, night, December,
through the well-kept park of the glamorous suicides,
neat pollarded elms
clubby fists of them against the sky.

## III.

Hope again. Habit
keeps you going,
the jailer brings breakfast,
good enough to eat.

You measure the sun
through the sextant of your cupped hands,
flesh telescope.
Today's the day they let you out.
You wipe your tin plate and wake.

No one to stop you but your feelings.
Carve a door, fit a handle to it,
throw it open and go forth
screaming Easter at every step, *da bin i!*
here I am and am and the roses
are to be happy with your company.

Here I am, girls, here I am
abbesses of so many secret convents
deep-daled in dragon woods,
here be I, with no roses,
no flowers at all but blossoming need.

*

You step along a way
you've been before
but this time you know it,
everything brings you to you.

*

The violent association
of thing with other thing
that we call thinking
requires an equally violent
disjunction applied by
waking mind – hauling
the rose out of roses—
and making the mind work
to dance modestly on
the other side of being,
we have a name for that too,
look close and you're doing it

and out of the smile comes
a kind of strutting forward
and out of the forward gait a road.
And you are the road.

## 24. K.491

So many wars
columns of soldiers
between stone columns
squeezed, march
into the city

the mind hovers around catastrophe

bees on linden flowers

the mind hovers hard around catastrophe

ripens, even tragedy
needs time,
and a man,

needs a man, always alone,
walks along.
A man walks along

a woman always attended
no matter how far she walks
can never outwalk her faithful suitor

fateful

some man
her shadow

   1. a woman can never walk alone
   2. a woman can never escape her shadow
   3. a man is the shadow of a woman.

and from these scant axioms
we have built our culture

columns
between
we also march

later, when the city falls.

*

Self in society,
the music flees,
everything you want is right here,
why run from that?

flight reflex
cadenzas of flightless birds

love sacrifices
heaped on broken altars

smoldering. Thou hast turn'd
the very air to incense
and made a church of every street

love poetry heavy left hand
translate this excitement
into the steady state of metal
which hides its crystal structure
in general sheen

is *ælf-scîn* I explained,
staggering potency of beauty
mere beauty locked in every single thing,

the hidden Powers of the world
time to release,

Bruno Schulz dying in the street
his head pillowed on the curb
at the feet of the beautiful invisible woman
he still served,

your skin, the shine.
Once he paused, drank,
tasted another person's lips
one time on that same cup

before him, he wonders,
wonders. Who. One column
is wonder, one is doubt.

Within their shadows
the city rises and falls,
armies come in and go out,
lovers simper in the shelter
of ordinary rock.

The street
where I was born
I have no other
body but the time
it comes from
a dreary little song
getting excited about itself
and then the shadow
slips down the column
hides under it
and it's noon

leaving us to wonder what language
our masters will try to make us speak next.

## II.

Such little things
commas in long sentences
wielding sense

to be little
is be everywhere
a servant of sensation

bird trill
and now the world
is just a dream of dead friends,

strange cigarettes
in a country they still smoke
and going downhill
(but I was staying)
they vanished into the ravine
underbrush and a bird

was crying, one that thrilled you
with what you called its baritone
cry, a bird I knew an octave up

but this one was now, low,
and forests had vanished, a friend
just one more dubious frontier,

daylight itself nothing but a customs post,
we're left alone with daylight fading
winter afternoon in opera season.

\*

You and your candles
me in my miner's cap:

we risk it
can we get through the dark

one more time and still not know
those odd potentates dressed up as animals

who wait for us there
trying to catch me by the sleeve

and make me turn, expose
my startled crime

to their glowing eyes
I have been running away from all my life.

## III.

That is the power here, beneath the lovely lyric is the lonely lover lover-less, idling down some path. And beneath that idleness a horror waits. What. This music is all about the horror underneath. And how to pass over, how to get to one more morning, safe once more from the demons of which I'm made. This is the truth now, music is Montaigne, music knows itself so well it can distract us both from what we know — don't we?— is going on down there, down here in me and thee, down here where music leads the way, crying, to all the dead friends, the gods who failed, the religions that just went away, the languages I couldn't learn, the houses that crumbled underneath me or the claustrophobic ones I fled, all the dead loves, all the doors, all the sensations, every feeling, all banked down there, my father's furnace, a bomber falls from the sky, everything I ever knew or felt died and went to heaven, and heaven is this hell to which the music summons, step by step, inexorable: What you have experienced is all you are, all you ever are. What you have done is all you will be. Don't look for some identity — you are a wave in water. And your friends are dead.

## 25. K.503

It always is another room
other people talking there
in other language

only the light comes through the door *Wiesbaden*
gold inflected from the chandeliers
a few real candles among electric tapers:

I am staring at and into the doorway
from across the empty lobby

revelers and stately gamblers
spilling their glamorous time

for what else have we to give?
A tree of poinsettias,

and Heine's low Taunus hills
just before Christmas north

and a camel lumbered down the street
its shabby wiseman saying nichts

not even ogling women, just
being there as a reminder
to bring something to our mind
but what? And what are they saying

all of them in their elegant languages
in the bright casino, why

can I see everybody and understand nothing?
Or is that the same as beauty itself

naked, no palaver, no resonance
but the intensity of presence

a child staring at bright lights
a woman in a blue dress, and the dress *shines?*

You go away five years and meditate
scarlet bracts on a dull tree, that's all,

child looking, dimly but intensely
conscious, the way children are,

his mother sobbing in another room,
someone lost, something missing,

one more thing he can't understand
I can't understand.

Be beautiful while it can.
They'll let you look your fill

and fail to speak. It is here: gold,
it really is, tell what happened,

what happened is what counts, old father,
ram in a thicket, sullen obedience,

rain on New Years, night of power,
camel in the market, Roman altar,

shadows by the museum and through them
a harlot passes, meets me at the river,

such a little river, speaks to me
one more sentence I'm ashamed to answer.

It is here, all round. It shimmers everywhere.
It is not meant for me to understand.

## II.

Is it rain?
Head lightly over music, ran,
no heard, rain,
like one more woodwind
offered to the sense of organic form,
could this be hearing,
the tiny copper filaments of the ear,
the brush that writes the sound upon the feelings,
rain on top of music?

\*

On the day Seven-Rain
an American day, a good day
to wear new clothes.
Break an old word
and take the new word out.

\*

As it gets true
the word gets short
till you can say it
in one breath,

no more, one breath
is all we need
to say it, to keep
the heart straight

if you have one
or find a new heart
if you lost the last
one you had at cards

or love or just
left it on the couch
next to you and then
lost sight of it when

you got up to sniff
at a wild rose or stroll
out in the yew hedge
the maze in moon.

## III.

On the last day of all the camel
plodded through the Christmas market
sluggish as a citizen, the Arab
at his side might not have been to so wise
but there he was. We watched,
safer than watching people. But those
are what we wanted. Those we love.
For them we came down from heaven
disguised as starlight, crept
into your mother's womb,

she thought she was just admiring
some amber in a jeweler's window
by the Grand Duke's garden
but it was us, inside her already,
admiring the whole world
through her shine, this amazing
arrival, the mother of all mothers,
she who is alive and wanted us
and we wanted her and there you are,
all of you, people in the winter street,
for you we came down from heaven
and sprawl in the gutter of your lewd
bodies, milk and blood and lymph
and god knows what inside you,
chyme and hormones and dreamy
chemicals sloshing round us we endure
the musical material that soon
will spring us out to be seen, moving
among you through the market,
hurrying sometimes, even whistling
when a little drunk, but never
saying a word, we have nothing
to report, we are here for your beauty,
people, casual people, there is no place
in the universe more beautiful than you.

# 26. K.537 "Coronation"

Would there be triumph here
without the name?

Leaves without a tree.

Questions seep into assertions,
a woman walks along a battlement
everything is always waiting

a nervous man at your elbow
wondering how fate brought you to this encounter

then babel starts
the ordinary conversation of the deliberate day.

Your hands are cold
Don't touch me

A raft is on the river
Come flee with me

into the intergovernmental agencies
that rule the stars

every human ruler is the shadow
of a crazed autarch elsewhere

sometimes up to good
just often enough for us to forget

he's mostly not.
She is.

Hence dance.
Long song.

We paint an image on the sunbeam
and kneel down to worship it
then sob when a cloud decides to come

at least a girl like you is kind
the neighbor's cat
the charitable volunteer

*

I am the rock where everything changes
but you have heard that line before,
I put the names of things in at random

to make you think the world is real
and my discourse somehow subtends it
sweater streetlight toaster full moon

but all those things are just the sounds
of themselves, assassins, museum replicas
you bought in the mail, mall, no, none,

there are no more words, and things
have had enough of your caress
so there's only one nationality left for you

a place to stand but there are no places
no island and no sea, a mere
continuity like the colors

you see when you press your eyes—

that is your homeland.
You never did care about the rock
and all those trees just fragrant obstacles

though sometimes in the endless plain
you were glad enough to nap in their shade
dreaming what?

a wordless thingless certainty
you woke from feeling comforted,
loved even, even known.

## II.

Red harbors.
Not here again,
so close to the frontier

my shadow
falls in the other country.
Doesn't it always, dear?

Yes, but it isn't always France.
There is a post that marks the border,
a goshawk on it, who could that be?

\*

I get afraid sometimes in the afternoon,

I ask myself why I'm doing what I'm doing
and not something else worthier or truer
but what could that be?

Why isn't the word I'm writing down a better word
telling a better story in a better tune,
I get afraid when I do what I do

because it's always me doing it
if it even really is,
I get afraid that I am no one

using someone's instruments
for some preposterous vivisection
of an imaginary animal,

afraid I'm no one using someone's words
to hide what I don't have to say,
sometimes in the afternoon

I get afraid of listening to my shadow
smiling or sneering at me from across the frontier
like a smart young man who's been reading Valéry.

## III.

Wake up it's yesterday
the light plays tricks
seeming through saplings—

nimbleness is all,
to get lost in thinking
and then spring out of it again

deer-footed, leaving neat pellets
inoffensive on the neighbor's lawn.

we walked by the river
on New Years Day
mist and clouds then finally
that circumstance
technically called Glory
coming at us from the southwest,
the sun herself clear over the hills
under the momentarily suspended clouds,

leap, from perceiving to perceiving,
leaving children to play on the cold grass
when we've drained it of our shadows.

Let everything begin again, Herod cried.
But there is no again, lord,
only the same children playing on the lawn
alive or dead,
or what lawn you left them,
Biafra, Somalia, Darfur,
just names, of course, the names
are the only things we really do know how to change.
Of course it's sad.
Music has to turn its back
on human misery
to exist at all. All
its nimbleness is fugitive.
Just as I here, for you, now,
running from my own shadow
show you how it's done.

## 27. K.595

Everything comes from far away
but the far away turns out to be
something deep inside here—

perhaps in the sense that someone who travels
is always more or less who he is
no matter where he goes,

or there are changes,
perceptions, character brought into the open,
he sees only what he is prepared to see,
or things always getting clearer
hidden in the lyric importunities of travel,
absurd lingering identities a place confers
stuck in your mind after you've left it,

remembering and all those stones
all the hues of that one color 'stone,'
Mozart on the road to Prague.

So it turns out that music is really about everything,
not perhaps every
thing, but everything of which statements can be made
that make any kind of sense

like: everything you are you take with you
on the road to Prague.
No road but a journey, a journée,
a day and a night of flickering experience,

everything you are comes with you,
cat and car and nurse and kid,
family bible and Britannica,
coal scuttle, parakeet, tea towel
porringer, plaster statue of Saint Lucy
holding her eyes in her hand,

easy, a traveler's mind is like a hand
nibbling at the keys of a piano
while the other hand holds a letter
someone wrote you, someone
is still writing you after all these years,
her too you take with you on the road to Prague,
*night and day keep working*
just to get to the next day,
next note, every decade an octave higher
until you pass the brink of human hearing.
Still you go on, you read the letter,
you fingers mumble some tuneless sequence,
one guess at a time, the fields are full of weather,
if it were Sunday we could stop for Mass.

But there's no stopping now,
you are committed to observation
and your insufferable patrons
demand verbose reports, tell all!
they told you, you do, you try
jumping down and running up the hill
but from the top see just another hill,
the road voracious for your company,
tell them everything, they have no lives
and need them to sing into their ears

as if they were living and the music
meant more than the wind does passing.
And it does. This thing you do
is about everything. You bring it with you
forward and forward till it is simple as you are.

## II.

There is a medicine
shaped like a leaf,
bring it to me.

There is a barrier
somewhere in the world
make sure the gate is locked.
Let no one break in
between one thought and the next—
if I weren't so close to the frontier
I wouldn't worry, or would I,
strangers keep trying to get in.

And they stand there some
mornings like leaves on a tree
just looking in at me

till I think I hear their thoughts
thinking, their terrible homeless
thoughts desperate for the Exile's
Dream, the little cottage where
for one little lifetime you
don't have to wonder *Where*
*shall it go next with me?*

The randoming. The curse of
fleeing, no one understands—
their thoughts make no more sense
than raindrops from the eaves, who are these
thinkings, who are these folk
against whom I have locked my door?

The question, so phrased,
romantically, despises easy answers.
But you know who they are.
If you were very young
you'd call them lovers,
bailiffs of the heart,
businessmen who come
waving bags of money,
offering again to write
your requiem for you.

## III.

Turkish fabric, Indian shawl, madder,
indigo, green and white of hellebore,
sun shining on them, winter sun
and amaryllis coming to a head,
signs, fiber, we wear clothes
just to put colors on our skin, colors
we change every day of the week as
Monday moon day white or silver,
Tuesday Mars day scarlet of blood,
so on, except on those full moon nights
when moonlight is green and frosts
the earth as if a snow had fallen

but no snow. We walk in colors
because of all things we trust color most,
and when colors fade we know how to weep
salt tears, mordant tears, when colors
fade we fade with them until love herself
brings us a new blue shirt
strong as the night
and we put on the sky.

There, that's where it's been going all along.
Enskyment of simple folk,
we, the children who believe everything we are told

because all everything is is what can be told
and there isn't anything on the ground or in the sky
you can't tell me about or I can't hear.

Remember that when you put on your new sweater,
the quiet one, the one I thought at first
too old for you, color of ancient Greek bronze
in sunlight, the one with little shiny beads sewn on
that draw the shape on you of something like leaves.

# COLOPHON

LISTENING THROUGH
was handset in InDesign CC.

The text font is BC *Figural*.

The display font is IBM *Plex*.

Book design & typesetting: Alessandro Segalini

Cover design: CMP

Cover image credit: Wolfgang Amadeus Mozart,
*Piano Concerto № 20 in D minor, K. 466 manuscript* page (1785)

Opening spread image credit: Wolfgang Amadeus Mozart,
*Piano Concerto № 8 in C major, K. 246 opening* page (1776)

LISTENING THROUGH
is published by Contra Mundum Press.

Contra Mundum Press    New York · London · Melbourne

# CONTRA MUNDUM PRESS

*Dedicated to the value & the indispensable importance of the individual voice, to works that test the boundaries of thought & experience.*

The primary aim of Contra Mundum is to publish translations of writers who in their use of form and style are *à rebours*, or who deviate significantly from more programmatic & spurious forms of experimentation. Such writing attests to the volatile nature of modernism. Our preference is for works that have not yet been translated into English, are out of print, or are poorly translated, for writers whose thinking & æsthetics are in opposition to timely or mainstream currents of thought, value systems, or moralities. We also reprint obscure and out-of-print works we consider significant but which have been forgotten, neglected, or overshadowed.

There are many works of fundamental significance to *Weltliteratur* (& *Weltkultur*) that still remain in relative oblivion, works that alter and disrupt standard circuits of thought — these warrant being encountered by the world at large. It is our aim to render them more visible.

For the complete list of forthcoming publications, please visit our website. To be added to our mailing list, send your name and email address to: info@contramundum.net

Contra Mundum Press
P.O. Box 1326
New York, NY 10276
USA

OTHER CONTRA MUNDUM PRESS TITLES

2012    *Gilgamesh*
Ghérasim Luca, *Self-Shadowing Prey*
Rainer J. Hanshe, *The Abdication*
Walter Jackson Bate, *Negative Capability*
Miklós Szentkuthy, *Marginalia on Casanova*
Fernando Pessoa, *Philosophical Essays*

2013    Elio Petri, *Writings on Cinema & Life*
Friedrich Nietzsche, *The Greek Music Drama*
Richard Foreman, *Plays with Films*
Louis-Auguste Blanqui, *Eternity by the Stars*
Miklós Szentkuthy, *Towards the One & Only Metaphor*
Josef Winkler, *When the Time Comes*

2014    William Wordsworth, *Fragments*
Josef Winkler, *Natura Morta*
Fernando Pessoa, *The Transformation Book*
Emilio Villa, *The Selected Poetry of Emilio Villa*
Robert Kelly, *A Voice Full of Cities*
Pier Paolo Pasolini, *The Divine Mimesis*
Miklós Szentkuthy, *Prae, Vol. 1*

2015    Federico Fellini, *Making a Film*
Robert Musil, *Thought Flights*
Sándor Tar, *Our Street*
Lorand Gaspar, *Earth Absolute*
Josef Winkler, *The Graveyard of Bitter Oranges*
Ferit Edgü, *Noone*
Jean-Jacques Rousseau, *Narcissus*
Ahmad Shamlu, *Born Upon the Dark Spear*

2016    Jean-Luc Godard, *Phrases*
Otto Dix, *Letters, Vol. 1*
Maura Del Serra, *Ladder of Oaths*
Pierre Senges, *The Major Refutation*
Charles Baudelaire, *My Heart Laid Bare & Other Texts*

2017    Joseph Kessel, *Army of Shadows*
Rainer J. Hanshe & Federico Gori, *Shattering the Muses*
Gérard Depardieu, *Innocent*
Claude Mouchard, *Entangled — Papers! — Notes*

| | | |
|---|---|---|
| 2018 | Miklós Szentkuthy, *Black Renaissance* | |
| | Adonis & Pierre Joris, *Conversations in the Pyrenees* | |
| 2019 | Charles Baudelaire, *Belgium Stripped Bare* | |
| | Robert Musil, *Unions* | |
| | Iceberg Slim, *Night Train to Sugar Hill* | |
| | Marquis de Sade, *Aline & Valcour* | |
| 2020 | *A City Full of Voices: Essays on the Work of Robert Kelly* | |
| | Rédoine Faïd, *Outlaw* | |
| | Carmelo Bene, *I Appeared to the Madonna* | |
| | Paul Celan, *Microliths They Are, Little Stones* | |
| | Zsuzsa Selyem, *It's Raining in Moscow* | |
| | Bérengère Viennot, *Trumpspeak* | |
| | Robert Musil, *Theater Symptoms* | |
| | Miklós Szentkuthy, *Chapter on Love* | |
| 2021 | Charles Baudelaire, *Paris Spleen* | |
| | Marguerite Duras, *The Darkroom* | |
| | Andrew Dickos, *Honor Among Thieves* | |
| | Pierre Senges, *Ahab (Sequels)* | |
| | Carmelo Bene, *Our Lady of the Turks* | |
| 2022 | Fernando Pessoa, *Writings on Art & Poetical Theory* | |
| | Miklós Szentkuthy, *Prae, Vol. 2* | |
| | Blixa Bargeld, *Europe Crosswise: A Litany* | |
| | Pierre Joris, *Always the Many, Never the One* | |
| | Robert Musil, *Literature & Politics* | |
| 2023 | Pierre Joris, *Interglacial Narrows* | |
| | Gabriele Tinti, *Bleedings — Incipit Tragœdia* | |
| | Évelyne Grossman, *The Creativity of the Crisis* | |
| | Rainer J. Hanshe, *Closing Melodies* | |
| | Kari Hukkila, *One Thousand & One* | |
| 2024 | Antonin Artaud, *Journey to Mexico* | |
| | Rainer J. Hanshe, *Dionysos Speed* | |
| | Amina Saïd, *Walking the Earth* | |
| | Léon-Paul Fargue, *High Solitude* | |
| | Gabor Schein, *Beyond the Cordons* | |
| | Marquis de Sade, *Stories, Tales, & Fables* | |
| 2025 | Sara Whym, *Dreamscapes I — Betrayals (101 & 202 Nights)* | |
| | Rainer J. Hanshe, *Humanimality* | |
| | Tahar Bekri, *The Desert at Dusk* | |

SOME FORTHCOMING TITLES

Scott Von, *Autopoesis*
Carmelo Bene, *Lorenzaccio* +

## AGRODOLCE SERIES ÆD

2020  Dejan Lukić, *The Oyster*
2022  Ugo Tognazzi, *The Injester*

# HYPERION
*On the Future of Æsthetics*   2006–PRESENT

To read samples and order current & back issues of *Hyperion*, visit contramundumpress.com/hyperion
Edited by Rainer J. Hanshe & Erika Mihálycsa (2014 ~)

CONTRA MUNDUM PRESS

is published by Rainer J. Hanshe
Typography & Design: Alessandro Segalini
Publicity & Marketing: Alexandra Gold
Ebook Design: Carlie R. Houser

# THE FUTURE OF KULCHUR

THE PROJECT

From major museums like the MoMA to art house cinemas such as Film Forum, cultural organizations do not sustain themselves from sales alone, but from subscriptions, donations, benefactors, and grants.

Since benefactors of Peggy Guggenheim's stature are rare to come by, and receiving large grants from major funding bodies is an infrequent and unreliable source of capital, we seek to further our venture through a form of modest support that is within everyone's reach.

Although esteemed, Contra Mundum is an independent boutique press with modest profit margins. In not having university, state, or institutional backing, other forms of sustenance are required to move us into the future.

Additionally, in the past decade, the reduction of the purchasing budgets across the nation of both public and private libraries has had a severe impact upon publishers, leading to significant decreases in sales, thereby necessitating the creation of alternative means of subsistence.

Because many of our books are translations, our desire for proper remuneration is a persistent point of concern. Even when translators receive grants for book projects, the amount is often insufficient to compensate for their efforts, and royalties, which trickle in slowly over years, are not a reliable source of compensation.

WHAT WILL BE DONE

With your participation we seek to offer writers and translators greater compensation for their work, and in a more expeditious manner.

Additionally, funds will be used to pay for translation rights, basic operating expenses of the press, and to represent our writers and translators at book fairs.

If the means exist, we will also create a translation residency, providing opportunities to both junior and more established translators, thereby furthering our cultural efforts.

Through a greater collective and the cultural commons of the world, we can band together to create this constellation and together function as a patron for the writers and artists published by CMP. We hope you will join us in this partnership.

Your patronage is an expression of your confidence and belief in visionary literary work that would otherwise be exiled from the Anglophone world. With bookstores and presses around the world struggling to survive, and many even closing, joining the Future of Kulchur allows you to be a part of an active force that forms a continuous & stable foundation which safeguards the longevity of Contra Mundum Press.

Endowed by your support, we can expand our poetics of hospitality by continuing to publish works from many different languages and reflect, welcome, and embrace the riches of other cultures throughout the world. To become a member of any of our Future of Kulchur tiers is to express your support of such cultural work, and to aid us in continuing it. A unified assemblage of individuals can make a modern Mæcenas and deepen access to radical works.

### THE OYSTER ($2/month)

- Three issues (PDFs) of your choice of our art journal, *Hyperion*.
- 15% discount on all purchases (for orders made directly through our site) during the subscription term (one year).
- Impact: $2 a month contributes to the cost to convert a title to an ebook and make it accessible to wider audiences.

### Paris Spleen ($5/month)

- Receive $35 worth of books or your choice from our back catalog.
- Three issues (PDFs) of your choice of our art journal, *Hyperion*.
- 18% discount on all purchases (for orders made directly through our site) during the subscription term (one year).
- Impact: $5 a month contributes to the cost purchasing new fonts for expanding the range of our typesetting palette.

### Gilgamesh ($10/month)

- Receive $70 worth books of your choice from our back catalog.
- 4 PDF issues of our magazine *Hyperion*.
- A quarterly newsletter with exclusive content such as interviews with authors or translators, excerpts from upcoming titles, publication news, and more.
- 20% discount on all merchandise (for orders made directly through our site) during the subscription term (one year).
- Select images of our books as they are being typeset.
- Impact: $10 a month contributes to the production and publication of *Hyperion*, encouraging critical engagement with art theory & æsthetics and ensuring we can pay our contributors.

### The Greek Music Drama ($25/month)

- Receive $215 worth of books.
- 5 PDF issues of *Hyperion* ($25 value).
- A quarterly newsletter with exclusive content such as interviews with authors or translators, excerpts from upcoming titles, publication news, and more.
- 25% discount (for orders made directly through our site) on all merchandise during the subscription term (one year).
- Impact: $25 a month contributes to the cost of designing and formatting a book.

### Citizen Above Suspicion ($50/month)

- Receive $525 worth of books.
- 6 PDF issues of *Hyperion* ($30 value).
- 1 tote.
- A quarterly newsletter with exclusive content such as interviews with authors or translators, excerpts from upcoming titles, publication news, and more.
- 30% discount on all merchandise (for orders made directly through our site) during the subscription term (one year).
- Select one forthcoming book from our catalog and receive it in advance of release to the general public.
- Impact: $50 a month contributes to editorial & proofreading fees.

### Casanova ($100/month)

- Receive $1040 worth of books.
- 7 PDF issues of *Hyperion* ($30 value).
- 1 tote.
- A quarterly newsletter with exclusive content such as interviews with authors or translators, excerpts from upcoming titles, publication news, and more.
- 35% discount on all merchandise (for orders made directly through our site) during the subscription term (one year).
- A signed typeset spread from two forthcoming books.
- Select two forthcoming books from our catalog and receive them in advance of release to the general public.
- Impact: $100 a month contributes to the cost of translating a book, therefore supporting a translator in their craft & bringing a new work & perspective to Anglophone audiences.

### Cybernetogamic Vampire ($200/month)

- Receive $2020 worth of books.
- 10 PDF issues of *Hyperion* ($50 value).
- 1 tote.
- A quarterly newsletter with exclusive content such as interviews with authors or translators, excerpts from upcoming titles, publication news, and more.
- 40% discount on all merchandise (for orders made directly through our site) during the subscription term (one year).
- A signed typeset spread from four of our forthcoming books.
- The listing of your name in the colophon to a forthcoming book of your choice.
- Select four forthcoming books from our catalog and receive them in advance of release to the general public.
- Impact: $200 a month contributes to general operating expenses of the press, paying for translation rights, and attending book fairs to represent our writers and translators and reach more readers around the world.

To join the Future of Kulchur, visit here:

contramundumpress.com/support-us

www.ingramcontent.com/pod-product-compliance
Lightning Source LLC
Chambersburg PA
CBHW020854160426
43192CB00007B/916